ROAD TO DIAGNOSIS

PARENT GUIDE:
ADVOCATING FOR
DIAGNOSIS FOR SPECIAL
NEEDS CHILDREN

ROAD TO DIAGNOSIS

PARENT GUIDE: ADVOCATING FOR DIAGNOSIS FOR SPECIAL NEEDS CHILDREN

CIANI HERBERT

Copyright © 2021, Ciani Herbert.
All rights reserved.
No part of this book may be used or reproduced in any manner whatsoever without written permission except in the case of brief quotations embodied in critical articles and reviews. Requests for authorization should be addressed to: cianiherbert@gmail.com

Cover design by Ciani Herbert
Interior layout and design by www.writingnights.org
Book preparation by Chad Robertson
Edited by Jacqueline Belanger, PhD.

ISBN: 978-0-578-92528-8
LIBRARY OF CONGRESS CATALOGING-IN-PUBLICATION DATA:
NAMES: Herbert, Ciani., author
TITLE: Road to Diagnosis – Parent Guide: Advocating For Diagnosis For Special Needs Children
DESCRIPTION: Independently Published, 2021
IDENTIFIERS: ISBN 9780578925288 (Perfect bound) |
SUBJECTS: | Non-Fiction | Special Needs Education| Early Intervention |
CLASSIFICATION: Pending
LC record pending

Independently Published
Printed in the United States of America.
Printed on acid-free paper.

Although the author and publisher have made every effort to ensure that the information in this book was correct at press time, neither author nor publisher assumes any liability to any party for any loss, damage, or disruption caused by errors or omissions, whether such errors or omissions result from negligence, accident, or any other cause. Both author and publisher hereby disclaim any liability to any party. Readers should contact their attorney to obtain advice before pursuing any course of action.

24 23 22 21 20 19 18 17 8 7 6 5 4 3 2 1

I dedicate this book to my daughter Cahsha and my Husband Cahtar.

"Be patient. You'll know when it's time for you to wake up and move ahead. Just by picking up this book, you've acknowledged your interest. That very acknowledgment will prompt change and carry you to the next step in the journey."
—RAM DASS

CONTENTS

DEDICATION	v
EPIGRAPH	vi
CONTENTS	vii
ACKNOWLEDGEMENTS	ix
Chapter 1 When I knew Something Was Wrong	1
Chapter 2 Noticing the Signs	4
Chapter 3 Questions Your Pediatrician Will Ask	7
Chapter 4 Questions to Ask your Child's Pediatrician	10
Chapter 5 How to Advocate for Diagnosis	12
Chapter 6 What is Early Intervention?	14
Chapter 7 Seeking a Specialist and Using your Insurance Company as an Ally	16
Chapter 8 Your First Appointment with the Psychologist	18
Chapter 9 What is Involved in Diagnostic Testing	19
Chapter 10 What Are the Assessments and What Do They Measure	20
Chapter 11 I Have a Diagnosis for My Child, Now What?	23
Chapter 12 What Treatment Options Are Available?	25
Applied Behavior Analysis Therapy (ABA)	25
DIR/Floortime	25
Bibliography	35
About the Author	37

ACKNOWLEDGEMENTS

I'd like to thank my cousin Jilliane Linton for pushing me to move forward with this idea to help other parents. Cahsha's godmother and my best, friend Jenifer Cortes, who continually makes me feel like I can do anything. Amina Abdul-Rahim, one of my oldest and greatest friends and one of the smartest ladies I know. You have taught me so much.

A special thanks to Aurelia Mack at Wings of Success and Erika Hartley Esq. Thank you all for keeping Cahsha, protecting Cahsha and covering her in your love.

CHAPTER 1

WHEN I KNEW SOMETHING WAS WRONG

When I became pregnant with my daughter, Cahsha, I had just turned 29 and was living in Houston, Texas. I had moved to Houston three years prior after graduating from college with my bachelor's degree in Sociology. It had taken me eight years to complete my undergraduate degree, and I was the first one in my family to achieve this major accomplishment. In addition to being a first-generation college student, I was a major procrastinator and was working multiple jobs while attending college (a terrible combination). Despite the obstacles, I was able to persist until I finished. Moving to Houston marked the start of a new chapter in my life. I was with the man with whom I would spend the rest of my life, and I was beginning my career in child protective services. Shortly after starting with child protective services, I was excited to learn I would be expecting a baby girl.

When I became pregnant with my daughter, everything changed. I would now be eating, thinking, and doing for two. The safety and well-being of my baby now took precedence over everything.

My daughter, Cahsha, was a full-term baby. There were some complications that resulted in an emergency C-section. However, after seven days of antibiotics, we were discharged. Cahsha showed typical signs of speech development. By 12 months, she had said her first words and was continuing to build her vocabulary. All of Cahsha's routine pediatrician visits within the first year of her birth had markers of a typical development. In fact, Cahsha was in the 90th percentile for all of her developmental domains.

When Cahsha was 22-months-old, she just stopped talking. It was like all her language had disappeared overnight. She could not say anything, except "up". She went from being a typically developing little girl, combining words to communicate and make requests to a girl who could only use the word "up". That was all that she could say. That was so scary for me, for *Us*. Not only did she lose her expressive language abilities but she also lost some of her receptive language. For instance, prior to her loss of language, when I would say to Cahsha, "Let's clean up our toys," she would pick up her toys and sing the clean-up song. After losing her language abilities, she no longer knew what "let's clean up our toys" meant.

I remember one day in particular. She was so upset, because she wanted *something*. To this day, I have no idea what that something was. But *she* knew what she wanted and was trying so hard to tell me, but the only word coming out was "up." She just cried. Then we cried, for what seemed like hours that day. When her dad came home, my daughter and I were just holding each other and crying. It was such a sad moment for both of us, because I think we both realized that we would never communicate like that again or at least not for a long time.

It would be another two years before Cahsha would be able to verbally communicate with me again. Even though she is now able to communicate verbally for some things, communicating most of her needs are still difficult. Cahsha, now 7 years old, still struggles with expressive communication. She can say individual words, and she can repeat phrases or sing songs. It is still very difficult for her to independently combine words into phrases to make a request or to express how she feels. The progress she has been able to make is solely attributed to therapy and individualized instruction. Without a formal diagnosis, Cahsha would not have had access to either of those.

Children like Cahsha, they have the ability to speak, but they lack the skills to effectively communicate. That is why early diagnosis and intervention are crucial on this journey. These are the first steps to accessing the necessary services for your child to reach their full potential.

I was fortunate to have previously worked in early childhood intervention with the Harris Center. In that role, I was exposed to all types of behaviors, interventions, and environmental components that influenced behavior. Every day, I saw and interacted with children whose behaviors were similar to those I started seeing in my own child. Had it not been for that experience, I might not have sought diagnosis for my child as soon as I did. It took two years, but my initial suspicions were finally confirmed with an official diagnosis. That confirmation strengthened my confidence in my maternal instincts and taught me to always follow those instincts.

It is my hope to help other parents like myself navigate this journey that starts with diagnosis.

CHAPTER 2

NOTICING THE SIGNS

- May not respond to their name.

- Does not point or look at objects to show interest by 18 months.

- Does not pretend play by 30 months.

- May avoid eye contact.

- May prefer to play alone.

- May have trouble understanding the feelings of others or talking about their own feelings.

- May have delayed speech and language skills.

- May have repetitive speech; repeating words or phrases over and over(known as Echolalia).

- May give unrelated answers to questions.

- May get upset by minor changes.

- May flap their hands, rock their body, or spin in circles.

- May have unusual reactions to the way some things sound, smell, look, taste or feel.

These are some of the signs considered "Red Flags" by the CDC. If you notice your child exhibiting any or all of these behaviors, tell your pediatrician and ask about diagnostic testing.

My daughter was exhibiting all of these signs when I initially made my concerns aware to my daughter's pediatrician. I notified him as soon as my daughter lost her language abilities. Cahsha had previously shown typically developing speech up until 22 months, so these signs were new. When I called Cahsha's name, she wouldn't respond. Cahsha would flap, spin in circles and repeat the same phrase, melody or sound for 10 minutes without stopping (repetitive speech). For almost a year, she only ate quesadillas, white rice, spaghetti, and oatmeal. She refused to eat anything else. She would only drink fruit punch and no water. Feeding/eating was incredibly difficult. Even if she was hungry, if it wasn't one of those four items, she would not eat.

At times, she would just burst into tears and cry for 30 minutes to an hour randomly. It appeared to happen randomly because I had no way of knowing how she was feeling. I didn't even know if *Cahsha* understood how she was feeling. Happy, sad, hungry are instinctive feelings, but the labels and constructs of these must be taught and understood. This involves another level of thinking: self-awareness. When a child like Cahsha exhibits these signs, it may be because they have not reached that level of thinking. Something that seems as simple as "I'm happy" or "I'm sad" is a little more difficult for her and children like her.

CHAPTER 3

QUESTIONS YOUR PEDIATRICIAN WILL ASK

It is helpful to prepare your answers to these questions before you meet with the pediatrician. That will help keep the appointment on track and allow you to get closer to a solution. Additionally, you will be asked these questions multiple times as you move closer to a diagnosis. Some schools and ABA centers may ask this as well.

- Were there any complications at birth?

- Was the child full term, premature, or overdue? (I was 1 week over due date)

- Did you breast feed, or did you formula feed?

- How old was your child when they took their first steps?

- How old was your child when they started talking?

- How many words are in your child's repertoire (i.e. how many words do they use or say)?

Be very descriptive about what their behavior looks like. Observe when your child shows a specific behavior or if there is a trigger for the behavior. Observe the different environments in which the behavior occurs (i.e. if your child has tantrums or different behaviors in different places.)

- When did you notice a change in your child's behavior?

- What was the change in your child's behavior?

- What does the behavior(s) look like?

- What does your child's play look like? (Do they line up their toys or play inappropriately?)

- Is your child's behavior different in different environments (ex. home, school, the community)?

- Bring videos of your child's behaviors, if they are hard to describe

- You also want to accurately describe your child's communicative abilities/disabilities. You will want to tell your pediatrician about how your child communicates, and how you communicate with your child.

Communication is broken down into a few general areas: expressive language, receptive language, pragmatic language, and functional communication.

Expressive language refers to the use of words, sentences, gestures, and/or writing to communicate with others. If your child is "non-verbal" or uses one-to-two-word utterances to communicate, they likely have difficulties with expressive language.

Receptive language refers to the understanding and comprehension of language that is heard or read. Some children like ours have difficulties understanding what is being said to them (e.g. following directions, understanding questions being asked of them, or finding/retrieving items by their description or name). An SLP (speech language pathologist) will conduct an evaluation to determine strengths and areas for improvement and will formulate a treatment plan to improve your child's communication skills.

Pragmatic language refers to how your child communicates or uses language in social settings when talking to one or multiple people, listening to others, responding to what they say and understanding what is going on.

Functional communication refers to how your child independently communicates their wants and needs and how they socialize with others. This is the most important area of communication for your child. It is essential that you try to remove yourself from the equation. Think about how your child would communicate with someone if you weren't there. What does that communication look like? Will someone else understand your child in the manner that they communicate?

CHAPTER 4

QUESTIONS TO ASK YOUR CHILD'S PEDIATRICIAN

- Ask the doctor to refer you to a psychologist who can perform diagnostic testing

- Ask the doctor for resources about children with Autism Spectrum Disorder (ASD) and Developmental Delays

- Ask for a referral for early intervention for your child

- If you already observe that your child is having difficulties with using eating utensils or motor planning (gross and fine), request a prescription for occupational therapy. You can begin OT as soon as you find a therapist.

- If you observe that your child is having difficulties with speaking and or communicating, request a prescription for speech therapy. (If your child is non-verbal, a speech therapist can advocate on your behalf and possibly help you get a communication device or system).

- o Some may require a recent hearing test prior to beginning speech therapy, to ensure the child is able to hear and process sound

- Also, if your child has difficulties eating or has a very limited diet (i.e., they will only eat chicken nuggets and rice), communicate this with your pediatrician, and request a referral to a speech therapist. The speech therapist may be able to help you expand your child's diet, introducing one new food at a time.

- If you observe that your child has mobility or muscle tone issues or is toe walking (walking on their tippy toes), request a prescription for physical therapy

Related services: Occupational therapy, Speech therapy and Physical therapy are more readily available. Services can begin in a matter of days to a few weeks while you wait for your child's diagnostic testing. Be sure to request and retrieve copies of evaluation reports for these services. Try to be as active in these sessions as you can, they will provide insight to your child's abilities and behaviors, which will be useful when you meet with the psychologist.

CHAPTER 5

HOW TO ADVOCATE FOR DIAGNOSIS

Look over the criteria for Autism Spectrum Disorder. https://www.autismspeaks.org/autism-diagnosis-criteria-dsm-5. This will be the defining criteria for your child's diagnosis. Make note of the defining characteristics or behaviors as they relate to your child. You want to be able to talk about how you observe your child, so you can best advocate for their needs.

Sometimes, the pediatrician may not agree with your observations, and they will dismiss and/or deny your request for referral. This happened to me. My daughter's pediatrician told me that my daughter "just needed time to develop…" and "some kids talk late." He completely disregarded the fact that she had been speaking previously.

I felt betrayed by my daughter's pediatrician for dismissing my concerns about my daughter's development. This was supposed to be the person to help with health issues and concerns for my child. It is disheartening to know there is something wrong with your child and to feel that nobody is listening or cares.

So, I had to do it myself. The first step I took was to contact my city's mental health authority and to request an evaluation for early intervention. After my daughter's evaluation with the mental health authority confirmed her developmental delay, I returned to my pediatrician with the evaluation report to substantiate my previously mentioned yet dismissed concerns. He apologized and provided support and available resources for my daughter's needs. Some doctors will be accommodating once you SHOW them that a delay is present. This is not always the case, and you may have to seek another pediatrician who can assist you. Sometimes we have family doctors who have been in our lives for many years, and preservation of that relationship is important. In the event that the pediatrician is not accepting or accommodating of your child's development, you will need to seek another pediatrician. At this point, what you will need to do will exceed the pediatrician's scope of practice. Talk with the pediatrician about a diagnostic testing referral, psychologists, developmental pediatricians, and pediatric neurologists that may be able to assist you with diagnostic testing.

CHAPTER 6

WHAT IS EARLY INTERVENTION?

Early intervention therapists may have more resources for what you need. Early intervention services are for children from birth to 3 years old who are suspected to have a developmental delay or Autism Spectrum Disorder. The pediatrics branch of your local hospital, your local department of education, or your pediatrician are initial points of contact to get referred to these programs. Some programs (like the Harris Center) allow the parent to make their own referral.

Typically, the early intervention therapist will evaluate your child in your home to determine if there is a developmental delay. If they determine there is a delay, you will qualify for either weekly or bi-weekly services. You can discuss with your early intervention therapist what options might be most helpful and also find out about community resources for your child.

My daughter was evaluated by the Harris Center in Houston, Texas. I worked with her therapist during every session, and we worked together to locate a psychologist to diagnose my daughter.

Remember to request and retrieve copies of all evaluations for your records. You will compile this with all other evaluation reports

CHAPTER 7

SEEKING A SPECIALIST AND USING YOUR INSURANCE COMPANY AS AN ALLY

If you have been unable to secure diagnostic testing from the resources your pediatrician, related services therapists, and early intervention therapist provided, your next step is contacting your insurance provider for assistance (which is what I did).

Ask your insurance carrier to speak with the mental health or Autism specialist. There are usually only 1-3 specialists for the region, so you may have to leave a message. They WILL call you back and can be a source of information necessary to navigate this process (e.g. newsletters, interviews and live calls with specialists and parents.) Use this opportunity you have with the specialist to ask any questions you may have about diagnosis and treatment. Be prepared with pen and paper. There will be an abundance of information, and you will want to gather as much information as you can. Don't think you'll just remember what they said. Write it down with a date.

Some insurance companies may not cover the cost of diagnosis.

Whether they will cover the diagnostic testing or not, ask them for a listing of the child psychologists, developmental pediatricians, and pediatric neurologists in your area. Call the specialists provided by your insurance company to see if they provide diagnostic assessment. I contacted all of the specialists given by my insurance company and out of 40 practices, three called me back. You MUST be persistent. Also, depending on the age of your child, some specialists may not provide testing. This happened to me. Some specialists won't evaluate before 5 years old. This was not due to anything discriminatory. Specialists are trying to practice ethically and responsibly.

Comprehensive diagnostic testing costs range from $800 – $3000, depending on the doctor. Sometimes psychologists and hospitals offer a sliding scale based on income, which may slide down to free for those with low income families.

GET ON THE WAITING LIST. Some places have waiting lists of up to 18 months for an appointment. When scheduling your appointment, let them know that you would also like to be on the cancellation list (if they have one). When people cancel or miss an appointment, they will sometimes try to fill the appointment with someone on the waiting list or cancellation list.

CHAPTER 8

YOUR FIRST APPOINTMENT WITH THE PSYCHOLOGIST

Your first appointment with the psychologist will likely include an observation of your child and a consultation with the parent(s) to find out more about your child's behaviors. This is where it is helpful to have prepared your answers to the aforementioned questions. Having all these items compiled together will help present your concerns in an organized manner and have a point of reference for the evaluator and psychologist. Sometimes the evaluator and the psychologist are not the same person. During my first appointment with the psychologist I compiled a binder with all the evaluations (speech therapy, occupational therapy, physical therapy and early intervention evaluation) and provided it to the psychologist. Remember your time during this appointment is somewhat limited. The psychologist will be briefly observing your child and listening to your concerns. It is your duty to make them all known at this time.

CHAPTER 9

WHAT IS INVOLVED IN DIAGNOSTIC TESTING

The diagnostic testing will be administered over 1-3 days. Your child will be given a battery of assessments as part of comprehensive diagnostic testing. After the assessment is completed, the psychologist will score and write up the diagnostic report. The diagnostic report will include a summary and analysis of their observations of your child, including characteristics and features that support their diagnosis. This report will also include your child's official diagnosis.

CHAPTER 10

WHAT ARE THE ASSESSMENTS AND WHAT DO THEY MEASURE

The psychologist may do a brief screening or conduct an IQ test to give the evaluator an idea of your child's age level of interactions and learning as part of your comprehensive evaluation. IQ tests that may be used are:

- Bayley-IV Scales of Infant and Toddler Development

- DAS-II Differential Ability Scales

- IDA-2 Infant Toddler Development Assessment

- Leiter-3 Nonverbal Intelligence Scale for Children

- Mullen Scales of Early Learning

- Standard-Binet (SB-5) Intelligence Tests

- UNIT-2 Universal Nonverbal Intelligence Test

- WISC-V Wechsler Intelligence Scale for Children

- WPPSI-IV – Wechsler Preschool and Primary Scale of Intelligence

There are many different assessments for Autism Spectrum Disorder. Here are some of the common assessments that are used:

- ASRS (Autism Spectrum Rating Scales)- 15 questions on the short form and the full form is 20 minutes for completion. This is a multi-informant measure for you and your child's teacher to complete that helps identify symptoms, behaviors and features of ASD in children and adolescents.

- ADOS-2 (Autism Diagnostic Observation Schedule) provides an accurate assessment and diagnosis of spectrum disorders across age, developmental level, and language skills.

- CARS (The Childhood Autism Rating Scale) is a scale used to assess the presence and severity of symptoms or behaviors of Autism Spectrum disorders for ages 2 and up. There is also a high functioning version.

- GARS-3 (Gilliam Autism Rating Scale) is a scale that measures social interaction, social communication, Emotional Responses, Cognitive style, and Maladaptive speech.

- ADI-R (Autism Diagnosis interview) focuses on behavior in three main areas: reciprocal social interaction, communication and language; and restricted and repetitive, stereotyped interests and behaviors. This test can be given to children and adults 18months and above.

- ABAS 3 (Adaptive Behavior Assessment System) measures the adaptive skills across the lifespan of individuals with developmental delays, Autism Spectrum Disorder, Intellectual disability, learning disabilities, neuropsychological disorders, and sensory or physical impairments.

- SRS-2 (Social Responsiveness Scale) identifies social impairment, degree of severity within the autism spectrum, and differentiating qualities from that which occur in other disorders. There is a parent and or teacher scale for ages 2.5 – 18 years old.

- DAYC-2 (Developmental Assessment of young children second edition) is used to identify possible delays in five different domains: physical development, cognition communication, social-emotional development, and adaptive behavior for children from birth through age 5.

- BASC-3 (Behavior Assessment System for Children 3) analyzes the child's behaviors from three perspectives; Parent rating scales, teacher rating scales and self (for children ages 6 to 7), child (ages 8 to 11), adolescent (ages 12 to 21), or college (ages 18 to 25). There is a Spanish version available for the child and adolescent forms only.

- VABS-III (Vineland) measures across three broad domains of adaptive functioning (Communication, Daily Living skills, and Socialization) as outlined by the American Association on Intellectual and Developmental Disabilities and by the DSM-5.

CHAPTER 11

I HAVE A DIAGNOSIS FOR MY CHILD, NOW WHAT?

After securing a diagnosis for your child, you may have to seek out insurance coverage for specific treatment. Refer to your notes from your conversation with the Autism specialist about coverage and treatment options. Therapy, like Applied Behavior Analysis (ABA), may not be covered by your insurance carrier. Presently, ABA therapy is not covered by Medicaid and some group insurance policies. You may choose to purchase a separate insurance policy for your child that covers the necessary treatment. If you have Medicaid, other related services (e.g., speech therapy, occupational therapy, physical therapy) will be covered in most cases.

The availability of therapies will depend on your coverage and mandates per your state. If you have to seek a child-only plan for treatment coverage for your child, it will be easier to get an insurance broker who will be able to walk you through the process and determine which insurance plan will be best for your child's needs. Try to find an insurance broker that specializes in special needs plans. They usually charge a fee of $100-$300 for the year. They can advise you if you have different employer plans to choose from and help you understand the billing paperwork once it starts coming in. An insurance broker can also help you find out what services are covered.

CHAPTER 12

WHAT TREATMENT OPTIONS ARE AVAILABLE?

APPLIED BEHAVIOR ANALYSIS THERAPY (ABA)

ABA is a set of principles that focus on changing behavior with a scientific approach. It seeks to identify and understand how behavior is affected by the environment and or other factors. It then uses that information to determine an appropriate and effective intervention. It seeks to identify how learning takes place with the individual. It establishes and enhances socially significant behaviors in a 1:1 setting.

DIR/FLOORTIME

The Developmental, Individual Difference, Relationship-based (DIR/Floortime) Model helps children open and close circles of communication while promoting social-emotional and intellectual development. This model uses 1:1 instruction or interactions on the floor or in the child's natural play environment to build communication, starting with narration of play. DIR/Floortime utilizes these practices to build upon and create relationships, and to support the organization of thoughts and feelings as part of communication-building.

Be very vigilant in seeking therapy options for your child. There are many services and therapies marketed to families like ours. This is why it is very important that you do some research. Discuss therapy and treatment options with your psychologist and insurance providers, even if you have Medicaid, to get an idea of what services are generally covered and what the options are for your state.

If you are offered medication for your child, research the medication and its side effects. Also, take into consideration the age of your child to determine if you think it will be appropriate or necessary for your child to be placed on the medication. Some medications introduced before 10 years old have the potential to cause organ damage in some cases of long-term use.

Once you have a diagnosis, if you are of low income, your child may be eligible to receive Social Security Disability Insurance (SSDI). SSDI can help pay for insurance premiums and copays and can provide Medicaid coverage. When applying for SSDI for your child, be sure to include the diagnostic report and other evaluations with your application. It is common to get denied the first time you apply. If that happens, you can file an appeal and reapply. Sometimes, after appealing the first time you will be awarded monthly financial assistance for your child. If you are initially denied and must appeal, whenever you are approved, payments will be retroactive from the date of your initial application.

SSDI is need-based and evaluated case by case, according to your state. The Social Security Administration (SSA) has their own formula of how they calculate what you will be eligible for. They also have a "resource limit" and income limit rules. You can review the rules on the SSA website. https://www.ssa.gov/benefits/disability/qualify.html You can also call to speak with a representative or make an appointment at your local Social Security Office. SSA: 1-800-772-1213 Tip: It is best to call first thing in the morning.

It is helpful to have your child with you at the appointment. When I had my appointment, my daughter started making very loud sounds and flapping while we were with the agent/interviewer. I turned my back to my daughter for five seconds to get a document the agent requested, and when I turned around my daughter was gone. My daughter had run almost out of the building before I caught her. When I returned to the agent, my interview was basically over and my application was approved. I am not encouraging you to purposely let you child perform behaviors that are harmful or dangerous to them in order to get SSDI, but it may be helpful for the interviewer to observe how your child's behavior is a barrier to learning and or communication, thus necessitating assistance for treatment.

If you are not Medicaid eligible already, you will be automatically Medicaid eligible once you start receiving SSDI. SSDI will also provide Supplemental Nutrition Assistance Program (SNAP) benefits for most states. Another benefit to being Medicaid eligible is you may be able to take advantage of Medicaid waiver programs provided by your state. Many states that have these programs have waiting lists of up to 11 years, so get on the waiting list NOW. Some states, like Texas, may require you to call every year to hold your child's place on the waiting list. States like Colorado, California, and Minnesota will compensate you as a full-time parent caregiver or Certified Nursing Assistant (CNA) for your child (under 18). In New York, you can hire family members as caregivers who are not residing in the home. Programs like these are valuable to families with little to no support outside of their immediate families. Special needs families often must sacrifice the income of one parent to care for their child. Many children's needs exceed what daycare, and some public schools are able to provide, making it necessary for the parent assume full time care of the child.

Research the available programs in your state to determine what will best fit the needs of your child.

When I lived in New York City, I had the Home and community-based services (HCBS) Medicaid waiver for my daughter when she was 4 years old. She qualified for a budget that paid for her after-school program, summer camp, respite staff, and other extracurricular activities that would otherwise be financially inaccessible.

Below you will find a compilation of Medicaid waiver programs provided by all participating states. Please seek out all assistance available for your children to create a nurturing environment for them to thrive across all domains.

State	Waiver Program	Age Requirement	Waitlist	Contact
Alabama	Intellectual disabilities (ID)	3	YES	(800) 361-4491
Alaska	IDD Waiver	No minimum age	NO	(877) 625-2372
Arizona	AHCCCS Section 1115 Demonstration Waiver	3	NO	(866) 229-5553
Arkansas	ACS OR DDS-ACS Waiver	No minimum age	10 YEARS	Referral line: (501) 683-5687 Apply for Children's Services: (501) 682-8158

California	CA HCBS Waiver IHSS program	0-36 months	NO	(916) 654-1888
Colorado	CHCBS Waiver program		5-7 years	(303) 866-7450
Connecticut	CT Home and Community Supports Waiver for Persons with Autism	3		(866) 433-8192
Delaware	DDDS Waiver	4	NO	(866) 552-5758
Florida	iBudget Florida Consumer Directed Care Plus (CDC+)	3	7	(850) 488-4257
Georgia	Comprehensive supports waiver	3	"Several years"	(706) 792-7741
Hawaii	DD/MR		NO	
Idaho	Children's DD	0-17	NO	(208) 239-6267 (208) 364-1906
Illinois	Children and Young Adults with Developmental Disabilities Support Waiver	3-21	5-7 years	(888) 376-8446
Indiana	Community Integration and Habilitation Waiver	5	5 years	(877) 218-3530 Apply at (800) 403-0864
Iowa	Intellectual Disabilities (ID) Children's Mental Health (CMH)		*Not for the Intellectual Disability Waiver	(877) 347-5678
Kansas	HCBS-I/DD	5	3-4 years	1-855-200-2372
Kentucky	Supports for Community Living (SCL) waiver and	No age requirement	SCL waiver has a waitlist	(502) 564-1647

	Michelle P waiver (MPW)			
Louisiana	Children's Choice waiver, The Supports Waiver, The Residential Options waiver	4	*Varies based on the service, program and funding source. Up to 10 years	(225) 342-0095
Maine	MaineCare, services for children with ID and/or /pervasive developmental disorders; consumer directed personal assistance services	5-20	NO	(800) 452-1926 or (207) 624-8000
Maryland	MD Waivers for children with Autism Spectrum Disorder	1-21	YES	(877) 463-3464 Or (410) 767-5600 for Maryland residents
Massachusetts	The Children's Home and Community-based Services waiver	3-9	*No. Must apply during open application period through MassHealth	(617) 727-5608
Michigan	Habilitation supports waiver and the children's waiver	No age restrictions	NO	(517) 373-3740 (517) 373-3678 (517) 241-3044
Minnesota	DD Waiver and Consumer support grant program		Depends on the services needed. Several years possibly	Intake worker (651) 554-6436 Medical assistance application (651) 554-5611

Mississippi	ID/DD waiver	No age requirement	Several months	(800) 421-2408
Missouri	Missouri Children with developmental disabilities (MOCDD) waiver, support waiver, partnership for hope and Autism Waiver	3-19	Depends upon prioritization score. Possibly years	(573) 751-4054
Montana	The children's Autism Waiver, The comprehensive waiver, and The community supports waiver	No age requirement	3 years	(406) 444-2995
Nebraska	The autism waiver, disabled children's program, disabled children's program	Varies by program, both young children and adults may qualify for services	2 years but varies by age and program	(800) 358-8802
Nevada	HCBW for persons with MR and related conditions	5	2 years but could be longer	(702) 486-7850
New Hampshire	In home supports for children with DD	No age requirement there are waivers for children and adults	1 year or more	(603) 225-4153
New Jersey	Medicaid community care (CCW) waiver Community resources for people with disabilities (CRPD) waiver	CRPD waiver children of any age	3-6 months	(888) 285-3036
New Mexico	Developmental	Varies by	Up to 10 years	(877) 696-1472

	disabilities waiver (DD waiver)	program but some may be available at birth	or more	
New York	OPWDD -HCBS Medicaid waiver	All ages eligible	NO	(631) 434-6000
North Carolina	Innovations waiver	All ages eligible	7-10 years	(919) 715-3197
North Dakota	HCBS Medicaid waiver, Autism spectrum disorder birth through four, and Traditional MR DD HCBS waiver	Spectrum Disorder: birth - 4 Traditional MR DD HCBS: No age restrictions	NO	(701) 328-2310
Ohio	Individual options waiver, level one waiver and self-empowered waiver	People of any age can receive the individual options; level one and self empowered waivers	Vary by county	(800) 617-6733
Oklahoma	In-home supports waiver, community waiver	3 years or older to qualify for most services	8 years	(866) 521-3571
Oregon	Comprehensive waiver, Support services waiver and behavioral model waiver	Support services waiver: 18 or older. Other waivers have no age requirement	NO	(503) 945-5811
Pennsylvania	The Autism waiver person/family	PFDS waiver: 3	7 or more years	(800) 692-7462

	directed support (PFDS) The autism waiver: 21 and older	years and older		
Rhode Island	The global consumer choice compact waiver	No age requirement	NO	(401) 462-4444
South Carolina	MR/DD waiver and Pervasive DD waiver	MR/DD waiver any age Pervasive DD waiver 3-10	4 years before getting on the MR/DD waiver varied for others	(800) 289-7012
South Dakota	The CHOICES Medicaid waiver program	CHOICES waiver has no age requirement	NO	(605) 773-3438
Tennessee	The statewide waiver (0128.R04) The Arlington waiver (0357.R02) and the Self determination waiver (0427.R01)	All ages may qualify	6 years	(800) 342-3145
Texas	The community living assistance and support services (CLASS) Program Home and community based services (HCS)	Any age	Up to 11 years	CLASS program (877) 438-5658 HCS program contact Medicaid hotline (800) 252-8623
Utah	Community Supports waiver	No age restrictions for the community supports waiver	5 years or more	(877) 568-0084
Vermont	Developmental disabilities services program (global	No age requirements for	Depends on level of need	Vermont benefit service center (800) 479-6151

	commitment to health 1115 Medicaid waiver)	developmental disabilities and home and community-based services		
Virginia	Intellectual disability (ID) waiver, The individual and family development disabilities support (IFDDS) waiver Elderly or disabled with consumer direction (EDCD)	IFDDS waiver 6 and older, ID waiver all ages EDCD All ages	Waiting lists vary by program up to several years	(804) 786-3921
Washington	Basic plus waiver, Children's intensive in-home behavioral supports (CIIBS) waiver, the core waiver	CIIBS waiver 8-17 all other waivers you must be 18 or older to qualify	2 years	(360) 725-3413
West Virginia	Intellectual/Developmental disabilities (I/DD) waiver	No age restrictions	Varied depending on slots that become available (125-175 slots)	(304) 356-4904
Wisconsin	The children's long-term support (CLTS) waivers consist of 3 waivers developmental disability (DD) severe emotional disturbance (SED) or physical disability (PD)	Age requirements vary by waiver	1 year	(608) 266-1865
Wyoming	Child DD waiver	0-20	1-3.5 years	(307) 777-7115

BIBLIOGRAPHY

Children's Hospital of Philadelphia. *"Speech, Language, and Communication"*. *Center for Autism Research*. 29, May 2020 Available at:
<https://www.carautismroadmap.org/speech-language-and-communication>

Constantino, John N. *"Social Responsiveness Scale, Second Edition (SRS-2)"*. 2012. Torrance, CA: Western Psychological Services.

"Disability Services & Waivers." 2020. MedicaidWaiver.org. Available at: <medicaidwaiver.org>.

Gilliam, James E. *"Gilliam Autism Rating Scale, Third Edition (GARS-3)"*. 2014. Austin, TX: Western Psychological Services.

Goldstein, S and Naglieri, J. A. *"Autism Spectrum Rating Scales (ASRS)"*. 2009. Tonawanda, NY: Multi-Health Systems, Inc.

Harrison, P and Oakland, T. *"Adaptive Behavior Assessment System, Third Edition (ABAS-3)"*. 2015. Torrance, CA: Western Psychological Services.

"How You Qualify | Disability Benefits | SSA". 2020. Social Security Administration. Available at: <https://www.ssa.gov/benefits/disability/qualify.html>.

Lord C., LeCouteur A., and Rutter M. *"Autism Diagnostic Interview-Revised (ADI-R)"*. 2015. Los Angeles: Western Psychological Services.

Lord C., Rutter M., DiLavore P.C., Risi S., Gotham K., and Bishop S. *"Autism Diagnostic Observation Schedule, Second Edition (ADOS-2)"*. 2012. Torrance, CA: Western Psychological Services.

Reynolds C. and Kamphaus R. *"Behavior Assessment System for Children, Third Edition (BASC-3)"*. 2015. Pearson Clinical.

Schopler E., Van Bourgondien M., Wellman G.J., and Love S.R., *"Childhood Autism Rating Scale, Second Edition (CARS-2)"*. 2010. Los Angeles: Western Psychological Services.

Signs & Symptoms | Autism Spectrum Disorder (ASD) | *Centers for Disease Control and Prevention*. 29 March 2021. Available at: <https://www.cdc.gov/ncbddd/autism/signs.html>.

Sparrow S.S., Cicchetti D.V., Saulnier C.A. *"Vineland Adaptive Behavior Scales, Third Edition (VINELAND-3)"*. 2016. Pearson Clinical.

Voress J.K., and Hammill D.D. *"Developmental Assessment of Young Children, Second Edition (DAYC-2)"* 2012. Pearson Clinical.

"What Is DIR?". 2020. Interdisciplinary Council on Development and Learning, Inc. Available at: <https://www.icdl.com/dir>.

ABOUT THE AUTHOR

Ciani Herbert was born and raised in New York City and moved to Texas after graduating with my Bachelor's degree in Sociology from Morgan State University. Upon moving to Texas, she gained experience in the mental health field as a behavior therapist for children on the Autism Spectrum aged 3-8 in early intervention. It was through this experience that Ciani was able to identify the behaviors she saw in her daughter. Ciani faced multiple difficulties in seeking diagnosis and intervention for her daughter. These difficulties prompted her to return to school for her Masters of Psychology in Applied Behavior Analysis at Capella University.

"It is my mission to enrich the lives of children and families promoting parent education, autism acceptance, inclusivity, and neurodiversity."

www.ingramcontent.com/pod-product-compliance
Lightning Source LLC
Chambersburg PA
CBHW070921180426
43192CB00038B/2151